Feeding

Hummingbirds

Nature's Way

Other books by Jack Aprill

Gardening Without Work

Garden Myths
Misconceptions and Old Wives' Tales

Feeding Hummingbirds Nature's Way

by **Jack Aprill**
designer and owner of
Leaming's Run Gardens

1845 Historic Route 9 in Swainton,
Cape May County, New Jersey
Exit 13 on the Garden State Parkway

Over 20 acres of spectacular flowers, ferns, lawns
and ponds displayed in 26 gardens.

**Leaming's Run Gardens and Colonial Farm
has the distinction of being
the largest annual garden in the United States, and
one of the top 10 gardens in the East.**

1st printing June 1996

ISBN 0-9641387-2-7

Printed in the United States of America
Garden State Printing
Fairfield, New Jersey

Skip Gladue, Editor
Helen-joe Owens, Production Director

Cover photo by Bill Reyna, Wayne, N.J.

To Emily:
Who can find a good woman?
She is precious beyond all things.
Her husband's heart trusts her completely.
She is his best reward.
Proverbs 32:10-11

ABOUT THE AUTHOR

Jack Aprill designed and created Leaming's Run Gardens, a labor of love which took five years of planning and work.

Leaming's Run Gardens have become world-class, with a totally different style from other gardens. In August, these gardens become a mecca for ruby-throated hummingbirds who come to feed before their long journey south.

In his earlier books, Jack Aprill describes gardening techniques which reduce work to virtually nothing. Those books reveal many of the secrets used in maintaining and developing his Leaming's Run Gardens.

In this book he explains the proper way to feed hummingbirds, so you may enjoy these delightful little hummers for years to come.

You may find the attitude of the author controversial, which will lead to many interesting discussions with your neighbors and friends.

Contents

Preface

I have observed hummingbirds for many, many years over thousands of hours, perhaps much more than anyone else. Hummingbirds are a delight to behold. They are not only exciting to watch in their natural state, but also very important to Leaming's Run Gardens, because they attract many visitors in August.

The information in this book is based entirely on my own observations and is not in any way influenced by previously-written articles.

You may recall, in my first two books we learned to ask, "How do you know?" Don't believe anything you read unless the author can prove he has actually observed the situation.

All the information in this book is from my observing hummingbirds and is easily checked by the reader by simply following the instructions given.

I believe that hummingbirds would not be decreasing in the numbers that they are if everyone understood their lifestyle. This book will be about ruby-throated hummingbirds (Archilochus colubris) because they are the only kind found east of the Mississippi River.

Things You May Not Know

Some facts about hummingbirds' natural habits which will help us follow their lifestyle in this book:

Hummingbirds hate each other.

In the many years I've watched hummingbirds, I have never observed a hummingbird seeing another without attacking it.

The male hates the female; the female hates the male, the fledglings hate each other and the adults hate the fledglings. In their world, if one hummingbird is seen with another and is not attacking it, it cannot go to Hummingbird Heaven. The only place you may see two hummingbirds together is at a feeder, and that is because they are sick from the feeder.

Don't feel sorry for their stark independence and their desire to be alone. This is the way they like it and this solitude is necessary to their lifestyle.

They eat alone, sleep alone, migrate alone and intend to keep it this way.

There is no such thing as a pair of hummingbirds.

Hummingbirds don't know what love is and are not interested in knowing. They mate entirely by instinct. When the light from increasing day length stimulates the female's ovaries, her instincts tell her it's mating time.

She wants only to be mated so she can be off to producing a family. No love lost there. Someone always asks at my Hummingbird Seminars, "How can they reproduce if they hate (a human value) each other?"

I tell them it isn't necessary to be in love to mate, or even to like one another. Humans always want to transfer their values to animals. They expect them to be in love, friendly, gregarious and sweet. The problem is that hummingbirds have never heard of these rules and don't abide by them.

Hummingbirds are extremely territorial.
They will defend their territory with tremendous fury to protect their food supply and attack any other hummingbird that enters into that territory.

Hummingbirds are animals (birds) not insects, and have the same nutritional requirements as other animals.
They *can not live on sugar*; no animal can. While all animals (including humans) use sugar for energy, *they need protein* to build muscles and good health.

Feeders can kill hummingbirds.
When the female hummingbird takes only sugar to her babies they die; no babies can live on just sugar. Since yeast and bacteria are always present in nature, sugar always turns to alcohol. Inasmuch as hummers never encounter alcohol in nature it's poison to them. **Alcohol can kill hummers instantly.**

I receive many calls from people who have found dead hummingbirds in their yards, always near feeders. I believe the **proliferation** of hummingbird feeders has resulted in a much-depleted population of these delightful little birds.

Hummingbirds need their natural environment to survive.
They are not porch birds.

Do Hummingbirds Need Red?

Just about everyone is convinced that hummingbirds are attracted only by red flowers. That's not true. They go readily to all colors. They need small tubular flowers, the color is unimportant.

> One day last year there were visitors at the Leaming's Run gazebo watching hummingbirds.
>
> The gazebo overlooks a long serpentine garden planted with red SALVIA. Everyone was watching the red garden (believing hummingbirds need red). Meanwhile on the left, at the edge of the red garden a small clump of white swamp AZALEA was blooming and being visited regularly by a hummingbird. The visitors didn't see it because they looked only at the red garden.

If you take time to observe, you will see hummingbirds on flowers of all colors. After you see them feed on all colors of flowers, you'll wonder why so many writers say they are attracted by red.

Remember, always ask *"How do you KNOW?"*

Now let's dig deeper into this red thing and you'll find out why it's not so. First, according to **Peterson's Wildflower Guide** there are only four red native wildflowers. They are TRUMPET CREEPER, BEE BALM, CARDINAL FLOWER and TRUMPET HONEYSUCKLE.

There are no fields of red flowers in the eastern United States. In fact, you seldom see any red wildflowers at all. That's because there are almost none. All our wildflowers are mauve (pink), yellow or white. I believe that hummingbirds would have starved to death if they had to depend only on red flowers. One of the first articles written about ruby-throated hummingbirds is in a huge book titled *Hummingbirds*, with data gathered in the field in 1849 by John Gould (1804-1881).

The following is a quote from this book.

> *A plant with a yellow flower grows in great luxuriance along the sides of creeks and rivers, and in low moist situations to a height of two or three feet and the flower, which is the size of a thimble, hangs in the shape of a cap of liberty above a luxuriant of green leaves.*
>
> *It is the Balsamina noli mi tangere [touch me not] of botanists and is the greatest favorite of all hummingbirds of all flowers.*

Notice there is no mention made of red; that's because there are only four red wildflowers in the eastern United States.

Let's review the four red wildflowers:

❖ The BEE BALM is a good hummingbird flower in areas where it blooms all August. However, in most areas its principal bloom is July, and its discontinuance of bloom will cause the hummingbirds to depart.

❖ The second is TRUMPET CREEPER, the most well-known. In some areas this blooms during August. However, this is a very aggressive vine. Homeowners might expect to lose their entire yard and have their house pushed into the street by TRUMPET CREEPER. Therefore, it is not a good choice.

4

❖ The **RED HONEYSUCKLE**, used by hummingbirds in their Spring migration north, is of little value since it doesn't supply food during the crucial feeding month of August when the birds are preparing to fly 500 miles at a time.

❖ The favorite flower of hummingbirds is the **CARDINAL FLOWER.**

Surprisingly, this is little known. Hummingbirds will leave all other kinds of flowers to feed on a **CARDINAL F LOWER.**

This is absolutely the best, and a perennial too. This beautiful plant blooms from the Gulf Coast to Quebec just as hummingbirds are feeding in August to mid-September. I believe this plant may be the reason for those who believe that hummingbirds prefer red.

Once upon a time, when our country was first settled, a mother said to her children, "Look! There is a hummingbird on the Lobelia cardinalis."
"Which one is that?" asked the children. "The red one," she replied. When the children grew up they sent their children to see the hummingbirds on the red flowers. A few generations later we looked for them only on red flowers, causing everyone to believe that hummingbirds preferred red flowers.

Hummingbirds in the Wild

If we all knew how hummingbirds live in nature we would try to enhance their natural environment instead of trying to change their habits.

Before the first settlers came over, what is now the eastern part of the United States was almost all forests, with an occasional open area created by the Indians. The only natural open areas were moist meadows and swamps.

To survive in this environment hummingbirds established a feeding territory. At water's edge, a hummingbird would select a **CARDINAL PLANT**, and camp by it, protecting it as his personal feeding territory.

Interestingly, this plant is fertilized by hummingbirds. While the **CARDINAL PLANT** provides the birds with the nectar (sugar) they need for energy, **the surrounding area provides the minute insects essential as a protein source.**

If you observe the plant while in bloom you will notice that a flower lasts for only one day, closing shut in the evening forever. A new one opens each day and closes each evening during August and early September, just when the hummingbirds need to feed heavily before their migration south.

For thousands of years hummingbirds had **never** been exposed to sugar (nectar) more than one day old. Because the flowers close each evening there was no chance for the nectar to ferment. Hummers' digestive systems can not deal with fermented sugar which is, in fact, alcohol. The slightest bit of alcohol is deadly to hummingbirds.

The Daily Life of Hummingbirds

Hummingbirds come to the U.S. in late March, arriving in Alabama about this time. They reach our area in Southern New Jersey about the third week in April. The little birds tend to follow the bloom of AZALEAS north and frequently will be seen on these bushes as they make a visit to your yard on their rush to their mating territory.

Filled with unbelievable belligerency, the male returns first to the same mating territory each year. Stopping briefly in your garden he gets a shot of nectar which supplies him with the energy he needs to defend his territory.

At this point it is important to distinguish between mating territory and feeding territory. These territories are usually different, however this is not a hard and fast rule.

To supply the male, female and young with sufficient food, Mother Nature sees that the territory varies in size. Where food is scarce, such as on mountains (or other difficult areas) the territory can be huge.

Remember, as soon as the male arrives in his territory he immediately proceeds to chase out all other hummers. His very favorite thing in life is to fight. There is no difference between the male and female in this regard, they are equally belligerent.

The female arrives perhaps a little later and seems to be a free agent, not necessarily returning to the same territory. The male hummer tries to attract her by spreading his tail, and trying to "flash" her.

In the male hummingbird's neck are small droplets of liquid called platelets, which, when in bright sun, refract a brilliant red flash. The flash is so bright it obscures the whole hummingbird. I have seen this only a few times in all the years I have been observing them.

Fortunately, two years ago our son Gregg went into our gardens, and filmed a half hour of the most perfect hummingbird video one could want.

Incidentally, a video camera is the easiest way to record hummingbirds. On Gregg's tape a hummingbird is perched on a four-foot stake facing the camera. The hummingbird turned his head part way into the sun and one third of his neck "flashed." When he turned his head the bright spot disappeared. Once you see a hummingbird flash you will never forget it. This is why the ruby-throated hummingbird is considered one of the most brilliantly-colored birds.

The male seems to know about this attraction and can be seen circling around the female to get into the sun to flash her. Like some males he thinks it's important that he appear big. Naturally, his macho antics probably don't impress most females that much.

The same circling occurs when two males fight. They will spiral up into the sky often out of human sight in a fascinating movement to flash their opponent. We seldom see this flash. When hummingbirds feed, their throats angle downward—not toward the sun.

Meanwhile, the female's ovaries are stimulated by the increasing light and instinct tells her it's time to have a family. She is mated with very little interest in the male and will likely attack him upon meeting him again and vice versa.

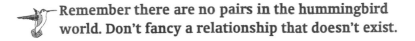**Remember there are no pairs in the hummingbird world. Don't fancy a relationship that doesn't exist.**

The male now rids his territory of all other humming-birds. During this period in June and July, hummingbirds seem to disappear. This is because their mating territories are large, and the male is racing around (the macho type that he is) looking for a fight and getting only enough nectar to carry on this fighting.

The female continues building her nest, in the lower story of trees. She usually lays two tiny eggs and incubates them in a cup-shaped nest she has built. She is not very visible during this period. At the end of July the young pop out of the nest

Keep in mind, almost as if computerized, Mother Nature has planned so there is ample food in each territory.

In early August instinct tells all hummingbirds it's time to head south. This is probably triggered by the decreasing light and approaching cold fronts. At any rate, Mother Nature says to the male hummingbird, "Now calm down! You've been flying around in a frenzy, fighting and eating very little. You're thin as a rail since you've been ingesting only sugar and now need to gain enough muscle to fly back to Mexico, Costa Rica or South America."

He now heads directly to his feeding territory in the first week of August, and the female who also is very thin does the same thing after giving all her food to her babies.

By close observation I have identified and named each hummingbird and its territory at Leaming's Run. For purposes of explaining their movements we will use our "Claude" as an example.

The hummingbirds that we saw in June and July usually go south to their feeding territories and are not the same ones that we will see in August. For explanation purposes, our

Claude may have his mating territory in Rochester, New York and when his instincts tell him it's time to head south, he flies in a beeline to his feeding territory at Leaming's Run in Cape May County. He will arrive here about August 4, come to the same territory, the same tree and even the same limb every year.

Hummingbirds prefer to perch on a dead limb, perhaps to see their territory better. We believe our Claude has returned here for about eight years. Unlike the many would-be experts that I've talked to over the years who claim they can tell one hummingbird from another, after seeing thousands of hummingbirds I can't tell one from another.

Since they don't have name tags I'll not be guilty of guaranteeing that this hummingbird is Claude. I do know if it isn't Claude, it is another hummingbird that won the battle and took over his territory. So for my purposes it's still Claude. He has been told by Mother Nature to sit quietly on his limb and his first priority is to not let another hummingbird in his sight.

He is to immediately attack any hummingbird that lands in his territory. After doing so, he returns to his limb and leaves it only to feed in his garden, getting a constant supply of nectar for energy and bugs for the protein he needs to build his muscles so in five weeks he can make the long, arduous migration south.

Hummers will return to the same limb year after year if they don't feed at a feeder between times. Fortunately, they come directly to their feeding territory and leave after the cooler weather when feeders do not pose so much of a hazard.

One of the interesting things about watching hummers in their natural habitat is that you can tell when they are ready to migrate. They tend to break their pattern of quietly dropping into the garden, and begin to do strange things like flying to a tree a distance away and returning. I often tell my wife Emily, "They're packing their bags." Sure enough a cold front comes through in a day or so, usually around the 10th to the 15th of September and off they go! You can visit our gardens after this time and there is not one to be seen.

Now this is the part that really disturbs me. Late September to mid-October, too many hummers straggle into our gardens. Some days quite a few can be seen too weak to reach the flowers and surely they will never make it south.

Twenty years ago the only hummingbirds seen this time of year were the old ones being eliminated by the migration as Nature wished, much fewer in number than now. Many of these dying birds fed only on sugar, their sugar high now gone, perish out of sight of the feeders they thought were a good and an easy source of food. If you could see these dying hummingbirds, you would be as disturbed as I am.

Feeders Can Kill Hummingbirds

You need to talk to me for only a few minutes to tell how unhappy I am about hummingbird feeders. We have more hummingbirds in our gardens than almost anywhere, and have no feeders.

Through my own observations, I hope to explain to you why hummingbird feeders are dangerous. Let us return to the wild, and study one of Nature's natural feeders, the CARDINAL FLOWER (Lobelia cardenalis). Just when they need great amounts of food this beautiful flower begins to bloom the first week of August and blooms until the hummingbirds leave in September.

The relationship between hummingbirds and CARDINAL FLOWERS has evolved over thousands of years. Hummingbirds will leave any other flower or feeder to go to a CARDINAL FLOWER.

If you look at this flower closely, you can see yesterday's closed bloom, today's bloom flowering and tomorrow's bloom in bud at the top.

Over thousands of years hummingbirds never have been exposed to nectar (sugar) that is more than one day old. They cannot deal with old sugar because it ferments and becomes alcohol. Looking up fermentation in the dictionary one finds: **change brought about by a fermentation which converts sugar to ethyl alcohol.** Alcohol is deadly to hummingbirds and it begins to form immediately in a feeder's sugar solutions, increasing rapidly in higher temperatures.

Because this subject is so controversial, I wrote to Donald W. Schaffner, Ph.D at Rutgers University, to verify the time it takes sugar to ferment. Rutgers University is renowned for its work with food preservatives and additives.

He replied:

"Sugar does not ferment by itself, it requires the presence of fermentative microbes like yeast and certain bacteria.

"If the right microbes are present fermentation will begin almost immediately at 85 to 90 degrees Fahrenheit, although the fermentation may not be apparent to the naked eye for several hours."

This letter indicates that we cannot be sure when fermentation begins. It could be immediately or later.

Are bacteria present? Of course. Take milk as an example. One need only to allow milk to stand at high temperatures to see it will sour rapidly. The same applies to sugar and water mixtures. Since the fermentation in feeders is hidden by red dye we cannot tell when it's present. This is the reason that pure sugar and water mixtures, such as maple syrup are clearly marked, "keep refrigerated."

Other sugar mixtures like pancake syrup are preserved by artificial additives and huge quantities of salt.

The following is a quote from John James Audubon (1785-1851) in John Gould's book on hummingbirds.

No sooner has the returning sun again introduced the vernal season, and caused millions to expand their leaves and blossoms to his genial beams, than the little hummingbird is seen advancing on fairy wings, carefully visiting every flower-cup, and, like a curious florist, removing from each the injurious insects that otherwise would, erelong, cause their beauteous petals to droop and decay. Poised in the air, it is observed peeping cautiously and with sparkling eye into their innermost recesses, whilst the ethereal motions of its pinions, so rapid and so light, appear to fan and cool the flower without injuring its fragile texture, and produce a delightful mummering sound, well adopting the insect to repose. This is the moment for the hummingbird to secure them.

Its long delicate bill enters the cup of the flower, and the protruded double tongue, delicately sensible, and imbued with a glutinous saliva, touches each insect in succession, and draws it from its lurching place, to be instantly swallowed. All this is done in a moment, and the bird, as it leaves the flower, sips so small a portion of its liquid honey, that the theft, we may suppose, is looked upon with grateful feeling by the flower, which is kindly relieved from the attack of her destroyers.

The prairies, the fields, the orchards and gardens, nay, the deepest shades of the forest, are all visited in their turn, and everywhere the little bird meets with pleasure and with food. Its gorgeous throat in beauty and brilliancy baffles all competition. Now it glows with fiery hue, and again is changed to the deepest velvet black. The upper parts of its delicate body are of resplendent changing green; and it throws itself through the air with a swiftness and vivacity hardly conceivable.

It moves from one flower to another like a gleam of light, upwards, downwards, to the right and to the left.

Please note in the quotation above the importance of insects in the hummingbird's diet. The high protein diet provided by the insects is not consistent with the feeder diet of pure sugar. With the feeder now placed on the porch, a window framing the total view of hummingbirds, where does the hummer get the insects in Audubon's description?

❖ Can they eat porch bugs?

❖ Whose porch were they on in Audubon's day?

❖ Can they pluck insects from the feeder as they did in Audubon's description?

I don't think so.

Then, the mother hummingbird comes to the feeder in July, and her babies die — no protein. Remember, hummingbirds have a tiny brain; they can't think; they do everything by instinct.

She doesn't say, "I have to go to the garden to get bugs for my babies." She takes the easy way out and returns to the feeder every two to five minutes.

In August, the hummers return to their feeding territories. We will return to Claude for our explanation. Let's assume I read all the ads for feeders, and hang a feeder up in Claude's territory (I hope not) and just let it stay there. Claude goes to the feeder, gets a big drink of fermented sugar water (alcohol) returns to his tree and falls to the ground dead.

Along comes a young hummingbird looking for a feeding territory and he can't believe he's not being attacked. Could this really be an open territory? What luck! He looks around at his new found food source and can't believe his eyes. He goes to the feeder and back to the tree and drops dead too. This can go on until either the feeder is sour enough for the birds to tell from the taste, or the feeder is empty.

Unattended feeders continue to devastate the hummingbird population while humans believe that the feeders are helpful.

Recommendations for sterilizing feeders are varied and confusing. The Audubon Society (much to their credit) recommends sterilizing a feeder every two or three days. Others recommend once a week, completing confusing the average person.

The problems the hummingbirds are facing are caused by innocent people who think they are helping them by using feeders.

Those who truly care about hummingbirds remove their feeders immediately upon learning about their danger to hummingbirds. Congratulations to this group; they ensure the future of hummingbirds.

Why put the hummingbirds at risk? I read a hummingbird book by a supposed hummer expert. The first quarter of the book discussed feeders. This was followed by a huge list of flowers, then a few facts about hummingbirds. This book is typical of books in which the writer probably has never watched them in their natural state and knows little about them.

He knew little about gardens too because the flower list was worthless. If you planted all his recommended flowers, you would have a great spring garden to feed the hummingbirds when they were speeding through your yard toward their mating territories, and nothing for them in August when they are settling into their feeding territories.

Feeding Hummingbirds Nature's Way

With all the controversy about the problems of feeders, it make sense to feed hummingbirds nature's way.

Feeding hummingbirds nature's way is also the easy way. **Nature's way is to have a garden.**

For the very simplest hummingbird garden you need only to replicate nature's system. A few CARDINAL FLOWERS are all you require. They will provide your resident hummingbird with all the food he needs if planted near or in a garden. CARDINAL FLOWER is a perennial; it grows from Georgia to northern Canada.

I will explain the propagation of this lovely plant later. Those of you who have read my first book, *Gardening Without Work*, by now have beautiful hummingbird gardens, a lot more time, and much more money.

But for those of you who continue to make gardening a lot of work I will describe to you how to make a hummingbird garden in your yard, spending a total of only 50 minutes. That's right — only 50 minutes a year — less time than it takes to sterilize a feeder twice. You'll have as many, or more hummingbirds in your yard, and they will be easy to see, a bonus of a beautiful garden, and healthy, safe hummingbirds.

Our sample garden will be 12 feet long and four feet wide. For this explanation, I assume you'll buy the plants. If you wish to start your own seed, please refer to my book "Gardening Without Work." You will remember we never sow seed outside.

After the danger of frost is over, buy some PETUNIAS, NICOTIANA, SALVIA and CARDINAL FLOWERS.

You will need a trowel and a gallon milk bottle of water. Start by planting about a foot from the entire outside edge one PETUNIA, one SALVIA, one PETUNIA, one SALVIA again about six inches apart. Dig a hole with your trowel, return the loose dirt to the hole, fill the hole with water and stir with the trowel to make a muddy puddle. Plunge the plant into the mud, merely displacing the mud with the plant, making sure the plant is set no deeper than it was in the flat.

You will quickly learn how large a hole you will need and will adopt our **muddy puddle system** to all planting from now on.

Down the center of your garden, length-wise, plant five CARDINAL FLOWERS two feet apart.

After the initial expense for the CARDINAL FLOWERS there will be no further cost because they are perennials. They will come up year after year and will be more beautiful than the previous year, year after year. Plant the remaining open space and between the CARDINAL FLOWERS with NICOTIANA and SALVIA eight inches apart. In shady areas you should substitute IMPATIENS for PETUNIAS.

As soon as you finish with your planting, apply two inches of fresh grass clippings between the plants over the entire garden.

Limit your application of grass clippings to about two inches to avoid nutrient loss and undesirable odor. Next week apply another two inches of grass clippings and continue to do this until the garden is filled up and there is no longer any room for the clippings. It should take only 20 minutes to plant your garden, 10 minutes a week to mulch it with grass clippings (for three weeks 30 minutes) for a total of 50 minutes and it's finished for the year.

Remove the PETUNIAS and NICOTIANA when they become scraggly. The SALVIA will fill these spaces; their bloom will continue all season.

If your garden has been covered by a commercial mulch such as ground bark or leaves your soil will be poor. Remove that mulch and put a circle of 10-10-10 fertilizer around each plant. Cover the fertilizer with grass clippings; don't bother to scratch it in. **It is likely your plants may need fertilizer again so just repeat this operation in about two to three weeks.**

You should not need to fertilize next year, as all the fertilization will be provided by the grass clippings.

 Remember, in my first book how I explained that in 18 years at Leaming's Run Gardens, we never weeded, never hoed, never bought fertilizer and never bought mulch.

This is absolutely true and this method will work in your garden as well. The garden just described will bloom from spring 'til frost and will attract hummingbirds and they will leave any other source of food to go to your garden.

The Hummingbird Barrel

For many years I have been recommending the garden I just described in the previous chapter and was stymied when folks said they had a stoned yard, no yard at all, only a porch or deck, lived in the woods with limited sun or didn't want to have a garden at all, but still loved hummingbirds.

Along came a smart young woman named Lynn, who after hearing the dangers of the feeder, went home and threw her feeder away, designed this barrel, and placed it on her deck. We call this Lynn's barrel. Later she returned to Leaming's Run excited and pleased because she had as many hummingbirds visiting on their way south as before. The barrel was much easier than maintaining the feeder and much safer for the hummingbirds.

She used half a wine barrel, drilled a few holes in the bottom for drainage. Next, she placed about six inches of Styrofoam popcorn in the bottom, about eight inches of any kind of dirt and then filled it to the top with Pro-mix$^{®}$, a seed starting medium available in most garden centers as are the barrels.

This mix is sterile and will not have weeds in it for some time. She planted two CARDINAL FLOWER plants in the center, and then about eight SALVIA plants around the edge, six to eight inches apart.

Water your barrel garden each week with a gallon of liquid fertilizer. If using Miracle-Gro$^{®}$, use one tablespoon to the gallon. Some additional water may be necessary in hot weather.

This simple barrel garden will provide you with the prettiest garden one could want; it blooms all season, guaranteed to attract hummingbirds.

After the initial investment, it will cost only the price of the SALVIA plants each spring, as the CARDINAL FLOWERS are perennial. This barrel can be placed anywhere, on your deck or in any slightly sunny area in your yard.

The only problem you may encounter is that your barrel may attract slugs. They are easily controlled with a little Slugetta®, a product readily available at your garden center and most hardware stores. It is harmless to the birds and need not be spread heavily. The barrel is also rabbit proof. My second book, *Myths, Misconceptions and Old Wives Tales*, covers slugs and snails in detail.

You may want to make your barrel more attractive by planting FUSCHIA between the SALVIA to hang down over the side and add more color to your barrel garden. Hummingbirds love FUSCHIA too. Remember, when you are growing flowers in any kind of container the best soil medium is Pro-Mix®; it will not compact and holds water well.

I have no information as to whether CARDINAL FLOWERS will winter over in a barrel in heavy frost areas. I have asked those who made barrel gardens north and west of here to let me know how their plants did over the winter. We know CARDINAL FLOWERS are very hardy all the way to northern Canada. Because we don't know how they will survive in a container, I recommend that you plant your CARDINAL FLOWERS in your yard during the winter season until you've had sufficient experience to determine their container hardiness. This garden will provide you with many hummingbirds, costs less than a feeder over the year, consumes little of your time, and, most important, feeds the hummers naturally.

Propagating Cardinal Flowers

If you wish to propagate CARDINAL FLOWERS follow these instructions carefully. In the fall after bloom, place a stake by each one with a bright ribbon attached. They almost disappear in the winter and have different leaves. The single biggest loss occurs when people chop them out in the spring, forgetting the plants were there. The stake will remind you where the plants are because in spring it looks like a weed.

After your CARDINAL FLOWERS bloom, you will notice a ball forms on the stem where the flowers were. These are the seed containers which are lined all the way up the stem. Each ball contains hundreds of seeds.

Gathering The Seeds

When the seed ball has turned brown, take a white No. 10 business envelope and squeeze the seed into the envelope. If the seeds are brown, they are ripe. If they are white, wait awhile until they are brown. You should get an envelope full of seed, if you empty each seed ball into the envelope. **Do not try to take the seed ball into the house because you will lose all of the seed.**

You will notice that the seeds are very tiny, almost too tiny to see. This is a problem. In nature these tiny seeds fall into the mud between the grass and water at the edge of a lake or pond. They lie in this little patch of mud, remaining wet for about three weeks. It takes three weeks for these seeds to sprout and they can not be dry at any time.

Sow the seeds in the fall if you'd like the plant to bloom the following August. When the plant is large enough to handle easily it can be planted outside, weather permitting.

27

Or it can be held in a plastic pot through the winter to be planted outside in the spring. However, if the seeds are sown in the spring you won't get a bloom until August of the following year.

Planting the Seeds

Use a regular flat with eight sections, each with six compartments. Fill each compartments with Pro-Mix®, hit the flat on a hard surface to settle the mix into the bottom of the compartments. Soak the flat with water thoroughly, and allow it to sit overnight. Do this for three or four nights.

When planting these tiny seeds, the Pro-Mix® must be very moist. Lightly tamp the Pro-Mix® down in each compartment; you can use a screwdriver handle. Do not pack it down; just smooth it. Now sprinkle the seeds on top and tamp them lightly into the mix with your screwdriver handle. Do not cover them with soil.

Next, cover each section with plastic wrap. Place the flat near a window in your house, and wait three weeks. The plastic will sweat at night and drop moisture onto the seeds, keeping them moist. Because the seeds are so tiny, and it is difficult to sow them thinly, you will have two to five hundred seedlings in each compartment.

As soon as the green is easily seen, remove the plastic, and water regularly. The seedlings will look like moss and sit there for a month, while you wonder if they **are ever** going to grow. Finally, they will make small leaves. When the leaves are an inch tall, separate them and plant them, one to a compartment, in another flat, using the same method as before.

Do not use all your seeds the first time. Save some for a second or third try. If your first batch fails, keep trying until you learn how. If you can get these seeds to grow you can consider yourself an expert. CARDINAL FLOWERS are some of the most difficult seeds to propagate. *Editor's Note: Now you tell me.*

How To Watch Hummingbirds

I believe that one of the major reasons that people use feeders is because folks find it difficult to see hummers in the wild. Once people learn to see them without a feeder, they'll never use a feeder again.

Don't even bother to look for hummingbirds until August, because they are very difficult to see before that. About the seventh of August, and it doesn't matter where you live, early in the morning look out at your garden, focusing on your **CARDINAL FLOWERS**. At first it will be difficult to spot the birds but be patient until you do.

One of two things will happen, if you keep your eyes on the hummer. Either another hummer will shoot out of the surrounding trees, viciously chase this one away or the one you are watching will return to perch in a nearby tree. Do not use binoculars while your hummer is in the garden because they fly so fast and it is necessary for you to see it return to the limb.

Now a number of new things have happened for you. You will have seen the hummer fly and you'll never forget its flight. Before this when you looked at your garden and you didn't know where to look for the hummingbird, he entered your garden in an area when you weren't looking and disappeared into the flowers without your knowing it. Now when you know its flight, you will see where it enters your garden and know exactly where to look.

Next, take your binoculars and look where your hummer went into the tree. Probably you can see it with your naked eye, but you can study it better with binoculars.

This is your hummingbird; you can name it. Your garden is its territory. Almost always it will be on its limb when not feeding or chasing an intruder away. Watch some tremendous fights and antics, watch the birds spiral into the air and watch them do things you never saw them do at a feeder.

Place your garden where you can see it from your patio or deck or put your barrel in a convenient place for viewing the birds. You will find hummers are easier to see on a CARDINAL FLOWER than at a feeder.

Other hummingbirds will continually try to steal its territory and you should see lots of activity. You will also draw hummers from your neighbors' feeders.

Also, you will be thrilled; your hummer will return year after year. You've likely saved its life by keeping it away from a feeder.

After hummers migrate they will be safe in Mexico because no one uses feeders there.

I welcome you to come to Leaming's Run. Come and sit in our gazebo and watch the hummingbirds do all the antics I've described.

It is my hope that the information I have shared with you will encourage you to plant a small garden and feed hummingbirds naturally and safely.

Jack Aprill

Frequently Asked Questions
and Their Answers

I often see hummingbirds in my garden that seem to go on a great variety of flowers. How can that be if hummingbirds prefer tubular flowers?

They are not hummingbirds but humming moths (SPHINX-MOTH). They behave as hummingbirds do, hovering and flitting about. Also they have a long beak and look very much like small hummers. They are easily identified because they have a hairy body like moths. They can be approached and hummingbirds can't, and the moths can be seen feeding together without fighting.

What time of day is best for viewing hummingbirds?

Early morning is the best although they need to feed all day because of their high metabalism.

How far can hummingbirds fly?

They can fly 500 miles non-stop. That is why the beeline flight from their mating tertrity to their feeding territory occurs. This also enables them to cross large bodies of water.

How fast do their wings beat?

About 80 beats per second (although I didn't count them personally).

Does noise bother hummingbirds?

Not normally. They seem to be immune to conversation or other normal noises such as a lawn mower, etc. They do dislike sharp snappy sounds and will flee from a camera shutter if close by.

How about movement?

It frightens them. Any movement implies danger. I have had hummers within inches of me by standing very still but while talking. You cannot walk toward them but must position yourself near your flower and stand still. They will come amazingly close.

How is the best way to see them?

Sit quietly. Have a conversation with a friend with little movement. My recommendation is to wait for five minutes (use your watch, it will seem like a long time).

My experience with small groups has been that they have difficulty waiting the five minutes and usually abandon the project, not seeing any birds.

What do I need to see them?

Patience, patience, patience, and a friend to help look. Talking is OK, moving is not. Field glasses are essential.

I'm sure I've seen hummingbirds on my zinnias, yet you say they need tubular flowers. How come?

Hummers can't think or remember very much. When he first arrives at your garden he doesn't know a tubular flower from a rose. The hummer will dart about testing until he finds the tubular flowers. Then he will camp near the tubular flowers and go directly to them.

Should I cut the old stems of my cardinal plant down in winter?
We use the dead stems to help us find the plants in spring.
But if you are annoyed by them, cut them off, no harm.

Why don't I hear more about feeding hummingbirds naturally?
I don't know. In a society that prefers to eat organic foods,
and is so concerned about the environment it seems strange
we would do the opposite with hummingbirds.

How else can I help the hummers?
A short tree near your garden helps them get close to their
food source.

Do I need to provide water?
My wife Emily saw a hummer bathing in a large dewdrop on
a grape leaf. Apparently they don't need much water if there
is dew. Surely dew will provide all the water necessary as will
nectar.

Should I feed hummers in spring?
Absolutely not. They need a heavy insect diet to ensure egg
fertility. Live insects provide a large part of their spring diet.

Directions to Leamings Run

Take Exit 13 on the Garden State Parkway. Turn right onto Avalon Boulevard, West to Route 9. Take another right at the traffic signal at Route 9, and travel North for one mile. Entrance to Leamings Run Gardens, 1845 Route 9 North, is on the left, just beyond a curve in the road.